Bar Studies Inspiration

DAILY CHRISTIAN DEVOTIONS FOR BAR MARATHON FROM START TO FINISH

IDA TYREE HYCHE

BALBOA.
PRESS

A DIVISION OF HAY HOUSE

Balboa Press books may be ordered through booksellers or by contacting:

Balboa Press
A Division of Hay House
1663 Liberty Drive
Bloomington, IN 47403
www.balboapress.com

1-(877) 407-4847
Because of the dynamic nature of the Internet, any web addresses or links contained in this book may have changed since publication and may no longer be valid. The views expressed in this work are solely those of the author and do not necessarily reflect the views of the publisher, and the publisher hereby disclaims any responsibility for them.

The author of this book does not dispense medical advice or prescribe the use of any technique as a form of treatment for physical, emotional, or medical problems without the advice of a physician, either directly or indirectly. The intent of the author is only to offer information of a general nature to help you in your quest for emotional and spiritual well-being. In the event you use any of the information in this book for yourself, which is your constitutional right, the author and the publisher assume no responsibility for your actions.

Any people depicted in stock imagery provided by Thinkstock are models, and such images are being used for illustrative purposes only.
Certain stock imagery © Thinkstock.

ISBN: 978-1-4525-7142-3 (sc)
ISBN: 978-1-4525-7144-7 (hc)
ISBN: 978-1-4525-7143-0 (e)

Library of Congress Control Number: 2013905812

Printed in the United States of America.
Balboa Press rev. date: 4/23/2013

For my Lawyer daughters:

Shade' Dixon, Geraldine Daniels, Ruby Brown, and Caroline Jackson; and my mother, Lue Birtha Crawford

TABLE OF CONTENTS

Acknowledgments

This book is, in no small measure, thanks to the Almighty God, along with the support and encouragement of my daughter, Shade', son-in-law, Jiwann Dixon, and husband, Albert. I extend gratitude to my nephew, Chris Crawford, Jr., for design and implementation of the iPhone App for this book. Many thanks to Ruby Brown for editing assistance. I am particularly thankful to them at Balboa Press that worked under very short deadlines to keep this book on schedule.

FOREWORD

IT WAS SOMETIME IN DECEMBER . . . my husband and I were in a Christian bookstore looking for a book to get his mother for Christmas. We came across the devotional section in the bookstore, so I started looking for a book for me. I love a good devotional book; but I needed one that spoke to me, about what I was going through at the moment. There were so many options—a daily devotional for women dealing with breast cancer, a daily devotional for mothers with adult children living in the house, etc. A couple months prior, I took the July bar exam and failed to pass by six points. I was getting ready to start studying for the February exam and I needed a devotional book that would encourage me and speak on the frustrations, situations, and emotions that I would soon face again when studying for the bar exam. That day in the bookstore, my husband kept saying, "this book is good, it speaks to women . . . or people going through a stressful period in their life." I told him, "They are okay but I wish that there was a book specifically catered to those persons taking the bar exam."

A couple months prior to this conversation with my husband, my mom, Ida Tyree Hyche, shared her idea about writing a Christian devotional for persons studying for the bar exam. At that time, it was just an idea. After the trip to the Christian bookstore, I mentioned to her all of the various devotional books I came across and none that spoke directly to me and others facing a rigorous study regime to pass the bar exam. I expressed my frustrations about the outcome of my previous exam, and how I really needed a good devotional book to read everyday to keep me sane and provide extra motivation. My mom replied, "well, how about I finish the book I am writing and I'll send you an excerpt every morning before you begin your daily study?"

So I was the test subject—the first person to read the book while studying for the bar. This book, even in its then incomplete form, was exactly what I was looking for. It spoke to specific emotions that I was feeling throughout the study process. All the procrastinators out there know that there is that moment when you can't procrastinate any longer. There is a devotion in this book that touches on that moment when you have to make sure that you are "buckling down" and studying. Anyone who has studied for the bar exam knows that it can be a constant battle to stay focused when you are doing the same thing over and over . . . and over. There are many devotions in this book that speak about staying focused. Also, at some point you hit a wall. You think that you can't take it any longer; you want your life back! I experienced that emotion plenty of times but just when I did, there was a devotion sent just at the right time to encourage me to keep pushing.

This book helped me in so many ways that it is difficult to explain them all. I am confident that it will do the same for you!

Shade' Alexandria Dixon
Cumberland School of Law, Samford University

INTRODUCTION

MANY PROFESSIONS HAVE ROBUST EXAMS. But taking the bar exam seems to be one of the most stressful times in a person's life, occasionally causing physical ailment or emotional breakdown. I am sure you have heard horror stories that only serve to instill or increase fear. After three years of law school, its accompanying huge student loan debt, and possibly an Attorney position with a law firm in hand riding on you passing the bar, it is no overstatement to say that bar exam study can be an extremely stressful experience. Our relationship with God can carry us through hectic, nerve-wracking circumstances. We merely have to ask, believe, and receive.

This book is a daily motivational devotion for bar exam study designed to cover your study period beginning after law school graduation to the last day of your bar exam, usually a two-month period. Begin your bar study marathon with Day One of your study session and end on the Day Two or Three of your bar exam as you finish your final lap (depending on whether your state exam is two or three days). *Bar Studies Inspiration* provides three to five-minute motivational devotions to promote quiet time with God before each day's study session. Your special time with God includes scripture, message, prayer, and a recommended song you can access on the internet to lift your spirit, calm and refresh your heart and mind with the strength to endure your bar study marathon. Or, if you are a musician, and you are familiar with a song, you can hum, sing, or play it on your favorite instrument.

While building my endurance for running in order to succeed in my Warrant Officer Basic Training, a personal trainer told me that I had to experience joy while running and celebrate my workout accomplishments one day at a time. That, essentially, is celebrating progress and feeling the energy it gives.

You, too, will be able to build on your daily accomplishments to finally create a great performance in your bar study marathon. By remaining stress-free, you can conserve the mental energy you will need for the more intense studying as weeks go by, ultimately strengthening you for the mental and physical agility needed on bar exam days. Expect your studies to be tiring. Expect it to be time-consuming. Most of all, expect Christ to be with you. The Holy Spirit, though unseen, works powerfully. I challenge you to seek Him, be encouraged and stay on track. If you are not a Christian, I trust this little devotional introduces you to Christ and that you will believe and accept Him as your Personal Savior.

~ *Ida Tyree Hyche* ~

Prayer for Preparation to Study

Dear Heavenly Father, you are my Shepherd.
I know you are with me throughout this extreme
marathon
of bar exam
study.
Give me peace of mind,
focus, understanding, insight,
and memory recall as
I prepare for this time of study.
Thank you for your blessing, gifts, and special favor.
I promise to give you the glory, honor, and praise.
In Jesus' name, Amen.

DAY 1

"Guiding Light"

"... and, lo, I am with you always, even unto the end of the world."
—Matthew 28:20b (King James Version)

THIS IS THE BEGINNING OF your marathon race, the bar exam. You are not alone in this race. Jesus is always with you. Before each bar study session, whisper a short prayer for discernment, and guidance.

Just as the disciples feared the thought of Jesus leaving them alone, you may feel a bit anxious about this journey to the bar exam. You can take comfort in Jesus' presence. Let Him be your guiding light. You will know when He's leading you. I can't tell you exactly how it will happen, but you will know.

PRAYER:

"God, our Father, I simply ask you and thank you for leading and guiding me through my Bar Exam studies. There is so much to study and remember, Lord, and half of it will not even be on the Bar Exam. Thank you for opening my heart and mind to receive legal wisdom and discernment through Your guidance. In Jesus' name, Amen."

SONG: "Savior, Like a Shepherd Lead Us (Blessed Jesus)",
by Leigh Nash

DAY 2

"Creating Your Own Darkness"

"You're blessed when you stay on course, walking steadily on the road revealed by God. You're blessed when you follow his directions, doing your best to find him. That's right—you don't go off on your own; you walk straight along the road he set. You, God, prescribed the right way to live; now you expect us to live it. Oh, that my steps might be steady, keeping to the course you set; Then I'd never have any regrets in comparing my life with your counsel. I thank you for speaking straight from your heart; I learn the pattern of your righteous ways. I'm going to do what you tell me to do; don't ever walk off and leave me."
—Psalm 119: 1-8 (The Message Version)

BAR EXAM STUDIES ARE INTENSE, requiring discipline and endurance. How did you get to this point in your life? You may wake up one morning and ask yourself, "Why am I here? I don't know if I really want to do this!" It is a natural response to question our choices and directions. God requires us to seek Him for directions in everything

3

we do. When we obey God, He guides us each step of the way and provides just what we need. Who said it would be easy? Often times that which we want the most may be harder to attain. Just don't miss your blessing.

In our Scripture David reflects over God's Excellency. David asks God to keep him on his prescribed course so he'd never have any regrets. Rightfully, he acknowledges God as the Light. The intensity of law school studies may lead you to lose sight of God's Light by shadowing or dimming it with your personal doubts, fears, inhibitions, and yes, occasional failures. My husband is prone to say, "sometimes we block our own light and wonder why it's dark." Get out of your light! Don't block your blessing. God is with you.

PRAYER:

"Father God, thank you for being with me all the way. Give me endurance when I want to stop my studies short of my daily schedule. Give me strength to say "no" with a loving heart to outside influences that will take me off schedule. Teach me to make my studies a happy time of learning Black Letter Law as I continue to learn Your law. In Jesus' name, Amen."

SONG: "He is With You", by Mandisa

DAY 3

"Forget All That!"

"But forget all that—it is nothing compared to what I am going to do. For I am
about to do something new. See, I have already begun! Do you
not see it? I will make a pathway through the wilderness.
I will create rivers in the dry wasteland."
—Isaiah 43:18-19 (NLT)

I FAILED THE BAR EXAM. THERE, I said it! But I was not ignorant, nor was I a failure. It did not matter how close I was to passing; I failed the exam. Yet, when I prepared to start the study process again, I had to forget past failures and claim the promises for the future.

The reality is some of us fall short, despite our best effort. Then we must pick ourselves up; and, as our Scripture says, "forget all that." Sometimes we forget that God is able to make all things work together for good. He can use even what we consider the worst occurrence in our life for good of His people and the progress of His purposes here on earth. If this is your subsequent time studying for the Bar exam, consider it your first, and claim His promise for your future. Stay on schedule . . . stay on the course. Reflect on lessons learned from past failures, but do not stay in the past. Look ahead. You can't run this marathon looking back.

PRAYER:

"Our Heavenly Father, Hallowed be Thy name! Help me to stay focused during my bar exam studies as I prepare myself to claim Your promise for my future. In Jesus' name, Amen."

SONG: "Victory is Mine!" by Dorothy Norwood

DAY 4

"Raising the Bar"

"I am The Lord, the God of all flesh. Is anything too hard for me?"
—Jeremiah 32:27 (NIV)

AN INQUISITIVE YOUNG GIRL, I remember asking my Mother, a deeply religious woman, "is there anything too hard for God, Mama?" She smiled, amazed, and told me God posed that same question to His prophet, Jeremiah. Noticing I still wanted an answer, Mama said, "No child, there's absolutely nothing too hard for God. Sometimes it's just hard for us to believe it."

Here, in our Scripture, the prophet Jeremiah had moments of doubt and questioning. God had given him a seemingly impossible command. Jeremiah's faith was challenged, but God responded to Jeremiah's questioning with this awesome declaration of His own all-powerfulness: *"Is anything too hard for me?"* But, wait! Moses did the same thing, actually arguing with God and giving excuses about why he couldn't possibly achieve the tasks God had for him! The good news is both men chose to

7

put their trust in the great power of God to turn perceived impossibilities into possibilities, thence successes.

As you prepare for your bar studies today, consider raising your expectations. Consider raising the bar, (pun intended). Do not cheat yourself. Study with conviction. Take your breaks, but stay on the track; whether your personal schedule or your commercial bar review course schedule. Believe in God's power to work wonders in your life.

God speaks directly to us. What we do in response to His directions proves what we believe about His ability. Do you think anything's too hard for God?

PRAYER:

"Lord, You're Amazing. Help me to raise my expectations and trust you more. In Jesus' name, Amen."

SONG: "How Great is Our God" by Chris Tomlin

DAY 5

Part One: Happiness with Imperfection

"The Law of the Lord is perfect"
(Psalm 19:7)

"Be perfect, therefore, as your heavenly Father is perfect."
(Matthew 5:48)

PERFECTIONISM PARALYZES AND KEEPS US from accomplishing our goals. The only perfect person who ever lived on this Earth is Jesus. Unless you are He, you're never going to be perfect on Earth in this sinful body.

Yes, Jesus commands: "Be perfect, therefore, as your heavenly Father is perfect." Here, Jesus is not only summing up His words concerning love, but His entire homily concerning God's Law, which is perfect and certainly demands perfection. Just because we, in our sinful nature, cannot attain perfection, does not mean that God should compromise His Law and allow imperfection. This is the standard of review for the Kingdom of God. This is the Law for the Kingdom of God. When we enter God's Kingdom, we will experience the gloriousness of a Kingdom that operates under His rule of law.

Until then, we are wedged with our sinful nature. We are imperfect people. While we may strive for God's perfection, we fail miserably.

Perfectionism impedes success. It encourages procrastination and inactivity for fear of failure, likely leading to anxiety. The problem often lies in our needing the ideal. When nothing but the best outcome is acceptable, disappointment is almost assured, reducing happiness on the journey and at journey's end. Why would we make the journey so stressfully unhappy by expecting perfection in an imperfect world?

PRAYER:

"O Perfect Father, thank you for sending us your Son, Jesus Christ, into an imperfect world, as an atonement for our sins and sinful nature. I'm not perfect, Father. But sometimes I place a great burden on myself to be perfect. Give me peace of mind to accept imperfection so I can release my bar exam study tension. In Jesus' name, Amen."

SONG: "Perfect People" by Natalie Grant.

DAY 6

Part Two: Happiness with Imperfection

"For I am confident of this very thing, that He who began a good work in you will perfect it until the day of Christ Jesus."
—Philippians 1:6

PERFECTIONISM CAN BE SELF-DESTRUCTIVE. HAVE the courage to be imperfect in a culture that idealizes perfection. The late Steve Jobs, and the celebrated Michael Jordan, understood how to learn from their mistakes and go on to greater triumphs. I'd like to think they were content living with imperfection, with no concern about judgment.

It is important to separate results from judgment. Strive for the results that are best for you, not letting your productivity be dictated by fear of others' judgment of you. Accept a broader form of excellence, rather than narrowly defining excellence by perfection. Study to learn

11

and understand, rather than to get a perfect score. A perfect score may follow, but the goal is to learn well.

In our featured scripture, Paul doesn't say that we will be perfect in and during this life, for our entire lives on Earth is a process of sanctification where we learn to walk in Christ's ways. Try trusting in a Perfect Christ to achieve happiness in an imperfect world.

PRAYER:

"Dear Heavenly Father, it's me again seeking your perfect guidance. I admit I want to score high on my bar exam. I want to score exceptional on my practice tests. Help me to focus on learning, understanding, practicing, memorizing and applying my legal knowledge so I can pass the bar exam. In Jesus' name, Amen."

SONG: "Tis So Sweet to Trust in Jesus!" by Casting Crowns

DAY 7

"Managing Time"

"Seek first the kingdom of God and His righteousness,
and all these things shall be added to you."
—Matthew 6:33 (NKJV)

TIME IS OUR MOST PRECIOUS resource, which is why we should use it wisely to fulfill God's purpose. In our Scripture, Jesus is saying that we need to set priorities in life. Our top priority as Christians is to seek Christ and everything that comes with His Glory. We should also set priorities in fulfilling our goals that shape us. Frankly, it is difficult to set priorities without effectively managing time.

Begin now managing your time for bar exam studies. A couple of months later, during bar exam week, you will not want to regret the time you wasted. Enhance time management by studying without distractions and disciplining yourself to turn down social options or engagements that conflict with your study plans, unless you need the break.

PRAYER:

"Dear Lord, please help me strike a healthy balance in my bar studies as I prioritize, plan, and implement my study plan. Please give me the ability to take care of myself in the process of fulfilling all of my roles. I realize how important it is to make good use of time, because you can never get back what you lose. I pray that I am able to prioritize my life and do the things that matter. In Jesus' name, Amen."

SONG: "I Shall Not Be Moved" by Mississippi John Hurt

DAY 8

"Run With A Goal In Mind"

"So I do not run without a goal. I fight like a boxer who is hitting something—not just the air."
1Corinthians 9:26 (NCV)

SETTING GOALS IS A PART of spiritual discipline. Paul speaks of self-discipline and challenges us to run the Christian life with focus. Setting goals in order to grow in our faith expands us, enabling us to be all God wants us to be.

Define your bar review goal. Certainly it is to pass the bar exam! Knowing what you want to achieve helps steer you in the right direction. The right direction may mean faithfully following your bar review course schedules, outlines, practice tests; or, it may mean organizing your own schedule and following it with self-discipline and diligence.

Pray. Tell Christ what you are trying to achieve because with Him all things are possible. Identify your goal and focus on it, without distractions, filtering everything to that one goal. Determine and execute the plan to reach your bar exam goal. Do not run this bar marathon without a goal. To do so is like a boxer just hitting air. Run with your goal in mind, claiming your blessing!

PRAYER:

"Our Heavenly Father, thank you for helping me achieve my goals. I claim my blessing. I know I must stick to my plan. I promise to give you all the honor, glory and praise. In Jesus' name, Amen."

SONG: "Go, Get it!" By Mary, Mary

DAY 9

"My Space"

"He leads me beside quiet waters. He restores my soul . . ."
—Psalms 23:2-3 (NASB)

THERE ARE BENEFITS FOR SPENDING time alone with God. We get to commune with our Heavenly Father, Lord and Creator! We get to feel God's presence, comfort, strength and calm as we meditate on His Words. He restores our souls! Start your day with that peaceful, quiet time, seeing yourself in that peaceful green valley. Ah-h-h, quiet time alone with God in your special space!

Find your special space for your bar studies. Create a sheltered environment for learning, one where you have permission to make mistakes. Rehearse. Practice. Review. Quiz yourself. Write outlines of model essay answers. During all these processes, tell your inner critic to take some time off, leaving you free to learn and practice without worrying.

PRAYER:

"Good morning, God! I'm ready for this once in a lifetime day! Thank you for giving me the opportunity to accept and enjoy its blessings! In Jesus' name, Amen."

SONG: "Like the Dew in the Morning" by Juanita Bynum

DAY 10

"In Spite of My Circumstances"

"But I want you to know, brethren, that the things which happened to me have actually turned out for the furtherance of the gospel."
—Philippians 1:12

WHEN PAUL WAS BESET WITH many circumstances or setbacks, he allowed the circumstances to simply make him stronger for the furtherance of the gospel. Crises, on the other hand, tend to make us fearful for our well-being. Rather than praising and trusting God for the faith and strength to see how He intends to shelter us through our circumstances, some of us become self-proclaimed masters of our fate fueled by fear and negativity. Our circumstances do not dictate our outcome. We must remain aligned with our purpose.

Stay aligned with your purpose and refuse to let circumstances and setbacks dictate your sighting as you study for the bar exam. When you surrender to circumstances, there are good days and bad days. You are at the mercy of what happens in your life on any given day. When surrendering to your purpose, there are good days *despite* the circumstances because you trust and understand that God gives you strength to endure and stay faithful.

PRAYER:

"Almighty God, I want to fulfill my purpose despite unfortunate circumstances, roadblocks, sidebars, and distractions. Thank you for your discernment. Thank you for making me stronger in spite of my circumstances. In Jesus' name, Amen."

SONG: "Stronger" by Mandisa

DAY 11

"Seek God's Glory"

*"So whether you eat or drink or whatever you do,
do it all for the glory of God."*
—1 Corinthians 10:31

SEEK GOD'S GLORY IN EVERYTHING you do. God wants every part of our lives to magnify Him; every task, decision, act, no matter how large or small. Even your bar exam studies.

How can you give glory to God with bar exam studies? By studying with the purpose of pursuing God's glory! When you disallow distractions during your scheduled study time, you glorify God. When you employ all your methods of studying, practicing, and preparing for the bar exam, you glorify God.

Studying for God's glory, you will not be tempted to drag your feet, procrastinate, or face your studies with misery. Instead, you will be praying and thanking God for another day to study to show yourself approved to become that attorney who will seek God's Glory and be a blessing to others.

PRAYER:

"Dear Heavenly Father. Help me see each day as an opportunity to glorify you in everything I do, so others can see a better picture of You through me. In Jesus' name, Amen."

SONG: "Do everything to the glory of God"
by Steven Curtis chapman

DAY 12

"Prioritize & Concentrate"

*"No, dear brothers and sisters, I have not achieved it, but I focus on this
one thing: Forgetting the past and looking forward to what lies ahead,
I press on to reach the end of the race and receive the heavenly prize for which
God, through Christ Jesus, is calling us."*
—Philippians 3:13-14 New Living Translation (NLT)

STAYING FOCUSED IN ANYTHING IS important. In the Book of Philippians, the Apostle Paul portrays absolute focus, narrowing his activities to those things that really mattered toward gaining intimacy with Christ. He prioritized and concentrated on the goal: The heavenly prize for which God, through Christ Jesus, was calling him.

Do you consider your pursuit of a license to practice Law a calling to fulfill God's purpose for your life? If so, are you prioritizing and concentrating to achieve that purpose? Make sure every activity on your schedule will pay off in the ability to recite black letter law, lest you waste valuable time. Constantly add to your inventory of black letter law by quizzing yourself, memorizing rules of law, and practicing application of law and analysis in essay writing. Merely recognizing law, "issue spotting," is ineffective if you cannot identify and analyze the rule of law.

Some activities feel like hard work but they don't help raise your grade, so they are a waste of time. Re-reading or re-typing notes is worthless if no new law remains in your memory. Plan for just one evening, or day, of relaxation a week, perhaps on Sunday. You can fully relax after you become a member of the bar. Grab every opportunity to practice memorizing rules of law when you are away from your study session; i.e., commute time, while sitting in a waiting room for an appointment, etc. Prioritize and concentrate. It's preparation for a marathon . . . you can go back to normalcy after receiving your prize. Like Paul, let go of the things that don't matter, develop a sharp focus, and fully concentrate on your bar study regime.

Prayer:

"Dear Heavenly Father. I really need your help to win my prize, a license to practice law from the state bar. Please help me develop a sharper focus and let go of the things that can wait. I pray for family support and understanding. In Jesus' name, Amen."

Song: "Stay Strong" by Newsboy

DAY 13

"Self-Discipline and Physical Stamina"

"But I discipline my body and bring it into subjection, lest when I have preached to others, I myself should become disqualified."
—1 Corinthians 9:27

It takes a lot more character to have the self-discipline to do something on your own than it does to be told what, where, when, and how to do something. Everything in life requires some sort of discipline. Even the apostle Paul was very much concerned about disciplining his own life in order to obtain eternal reward. In our scripture, Paul not only challenges us to run with prioritization and concentration (see Day 12), but to maintain self-discipline. During my years as an Army Reserve officer, I learned that self-discipline breeds a sense of confidence, responsibility for self and others, and pride in performing well.

We can apply the same character of self-discipline in our bar studies. Track-and-field Olympian, Jesse Owens, once said, "we all have dreams. But in order to make dreams become a reality, it takes an awful lot of determination, dedication, self-discipline, and effort." Many people have aspirations they will never realize, goals they will never achieve, dreams that will never emerge simply because they have no self-discipline. If you want to be really ready for your bar exam marathon, it's going to entail obstinately pushing past your comfort zone, frustrations, struggles, setbacks and failures. Every worthwhile accomplishment costs.

The bar exam is a physical challenge. Perform strenuous physical exercise for 30 minutes to one hour every day. While you may be tempted to skip exercise, don't fret; you can use flash cards for black letter law memorization while you exercise. Walk/run the dog, treadmill, or track, reciting black letter law. Climb up to the roof in your building and run downstairs or run up and down stairs in your home reciting black letter law! Exercise, like prayer, makes you feel better and more receptive to learn the law, giving you the strength to complete the exam. Maintaining physical stamina makes you cheerful, sane, mentally sharp, and able to sleep well.

PRAYER:

"Lord, keep me day by day in Your good and perfect way. Thank you for the strength and courage to persevere. In Jesus' name, Amen."

SONG: "Courageous" by Casting Crowns

DAY 14

"The Cost"

"For which of you, desiring to build a tower, does not first sit down and count the cost, whether he has enough to complete it? Otherwise, when he has laid a foundation and is not able to finish, all who see it begin to mock him, saying, 'This man began to build and was not able to finish.'"
—Luke 14:28-30 (ESV)

THERE IS A SAYING, "YOU need to hope for the best—but plan for the worst," which provides much wisdom. But the greatest wisdom is found in Jesus' words in our Scripture. Jesus speaks about planning. He tells us that it is important to properly count the cost of an endeavor in order to finish successfully. God not only wants us to start something, He wants us to finish it.

Now that you have started your race to the bar exam, God expects you to finish it, and finish well. Once you start, accept the cost of giving up some old habits, free time, and other distractions. There is a price to pay for bar exam studies. If you want to succeed, you must plan to count the cost. The prospect of becoming an attorney is a new exciting dimension in your life. But it has a down side: A demanding sacrifice and commitment to bar exam studies. Understand the requirement for your total and complete dedication to praying, studying, practicing, and following your schedule.

PRAYER:

"Dear Lord, thank You for Your examples of the cost of discipleship. Now, Lord, I want to also use Your wisdom as I plan and commit to my bar exam studies. In Jesus' name, Amen."

SONG: "Jesus Paid it All" by Kristian Stanfill

DAY 15

"You're Looking at a Masterpiece"

"For we are God's masterpiece. He has created us anew in Christ Jesus, so we can do the good things He planned for us long ago."
—Ephesians 2:10

TRAVELING FROM A MEETING IN Colorado Springs, CO to my hotel one summer day, I saw the most spectacular, beautiful, perfect rainbow. I was so awestricken; I took a picture and shared it on Facebook and Twitter. "Look at God's masterpiece!", I exclaimed. But, the truth is, you and I are God's greatest work of art. When God made us, He made a masterpiece. Many of us are just struggling to see the value in the masterpiece God made.

Acknowledge that you are important and responsible for adding value to the world that surrounds you. God created you for His good purpose, and, without a doubt, you are His masterpiece!

Are you adding value to the world around you as you study for the bar exam? Absolutely! Studying for the bar can be tremendously boring, stressful and frustrating. But, when you want to give up, look in the mirror at God's Masterpiece. Remember the old bumper sticker saying, "God don't make no junk!" See that masterpiece as the best young lawyer your State Bar will be privileged to admit. You want to be able to say, on the day after the exam, "I truly gave it my best, no regrets."

PRAYER:

"Dear Heavenly Father, thank you for making me your prized creation! Bless you, Lord, I praise your holy name. In Jesus' name, Amen."

SONG: "Bless The Lord, O My Soul" by Matt Redmon

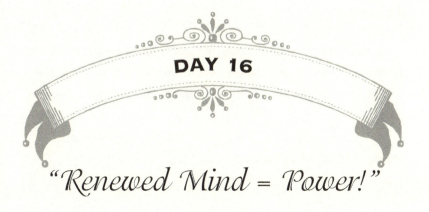

DAY 16

"Renewed Mind = Power!"

*"And do not be conformed to this world, but be transformed by the renewing of
your mind, that you may prove what is that good
and acceptable and perfect will of God."*
—Romans 12:2 (NKJV)

A RENEWED MIND IS ONE THAT sheds negative or sinful thoughts that diminish God's Spirit. A renewal of the mind in a Christ-like way will change our lives and the way we approach challenges. It takes confessing, repenting, and burying those negative thoughts.

If you have negative thoughts lingering in the back of your mind about your ability to persevere in your bar studies, and pass the exam, SHED them, now! Enjoy your studies, despite its tedious journey. By now you should be nearing your "second wind" in this race to the bar exam. Keep your pace, don't slow down, the mind may be getting just a little tired now, but don't stop, ENDURE! It is imperative that you keep your mind renewed with Christ-like thoughts . . . remember, "God has

31

not given us a spirit of fear and timidity, but of power, love, and self-discipline." (2Timothy 1:7).

Prayer:

"Dear Heavenly Father, I pray for the ability and strength to confess thoughts I have that don't reflect your Spirit. Not just for bar studies, Lord, but as a sacrificial Christian seeking to fulfill my purpose. In Jesus' name, Amen."

Song: "All to Jesus, I surrender."

DAY 17

"Don't Be Afraid"

"Do not fear, for I am with you."
—Isaiah 41:10

I REMEMBER BEING LITERALLY AFRAID OF the bar exam. It was the big "unknown" variable that wanted more of my knowledge than I could possibly give! What if I'm missing something in my studies? What if, this? What if, that? So, I literally succumbed to the fears behind the "what ifs" of my great unknown and successfully failed the bar exam.

King David said, "What time I am afraid, I will . . . trust . . . in You" (Psalm 56:3). Timothy said God has not given us a spirit of fear (2Timothy:7). Joyce Meyer once said "face fear and find freedom." God says, "Fear not, for I am with you" (Isaiah 41:10). Jesus gives a wonderful expression of God's love overcoming fear in 1 John 4: 1-21.

Fear is something that God has ordained for His glory. Proverbs 1:7 tells us, "The fear of the Lord is the beginning of knowledge, but fools despise wisdom and discipline." God's will is not for us to be afraid but to find courage and strength in the Lord. Our fear should only be of Him.

It takes calm, discipline, self-assurance, and faith, along with precise studies, for the bar exam. I admonish you to find enjoyment in the process. Use your practice tests to gauge your level of understanding, not to instill fear.

Jesus frequently greeted his friends with the salutation, "Don't be afraid." I am closing this inspiration with the same words: "Don't be afraid."

PRAYER:

"Dear Heavenly Father, thank you for helping me to face fear boldly with faith, courage, and the assurance of Your love, in all aspects of my life. In Jesus' name, Amen."

SONG: "Hello Fear" by Kirk Franklin

DAY 18

"The Sanity Rule: 4 Ps"

"Therefore, humble yourselves under the mighty hand of God, that He
may exalt you in due time, casting all your anxiety on
Him because He cares for you."
—1Peter 5:6-7 (NKJV)

I REMEMBER A YOUNG LADY HAVING a severe panic attack during the bar exam and paramedics had to come to her aid. This happened on the second day in the afternoon. Sadly, she didn't return on the third day.

Panic can have disastrous effects on performance. Foremost, panicking serves to inhibit our memory from functioning well. The more anxious we are about remembering something, the less likely we are to remember it. If you panic, you will not read questions carefully enough to pick the correct answer. Or, worst, you may get the increased heart rate, beads of sweat, chest tightness, upset stomach that come with panic attacks and not function well.

In our scripture, Peter reminds us that leaders are to humble themselves by casting all cares on God. Leaders also prepare and study to show themselves approved.

Remember this rule for bar exam sanity: Preparation and peaceful mind prevents panic (PPPP). Enjoy your studies!

PRAYER:

"Dear Heavenly Father, I have a job riding on my passing the bar exam. I want to remember all I study, but sometimes I fall short. Please give me the ability to analyze questions sufficiently enough to select correct responses. Thank you for your love, mercy, and grace; for being the One on which I can cast all my cares. In Jesus' name, Amen."

SONG: "Cast all Your Cares" by Gary Oliver

"Fruit of the Holy Spirit: JOY"

"But the fruit of the Spirit is love, joy, peace, forbearance, kindness, goodness,
faithfulness, gentleness and self-control.
Against such things there is no law."
—Galatians 5:22-23

ARE YOU HAPPY? THE COMMON belief is that happiness is an achievement that we can hold on to and hang on our wall. Lasting happiness is elusive. If life is based on obtaining happiness, then we will always fall short because life is always changing.

The Bible speaks more often of joy than of being happy. Happiness is a glad feeling that depends on something good happening. Joy, on the other hand, is a strong foundation that supports a variety of healthy emotions, including happiness. The evidence of joy is gratitude, contentment, optimism, a sense of freedom and other positive attitudes.

To grow in joy, we must shake off self-pity, self-centeredness, and self-absorption. When you complete your bar studies and become a Lawyer, I encourage you to render pro bono service as a way of giving back to your community. There is joy in service to others. God created us to give. Joy flourishes in our lives by loving Jesus, others, and ourselves. Hence, JOY (Jesus, Others, You).

PRAYER:

"Dear Heavenly Father, thank you for unconditional, everlasting JOY. In Jesus' name, Amen."

SONG: "This Joy I Have" by Shirley Caesar

DAY 20

"Flash!"

"But recall the former days in which, after you were illuminated,
you endured a great struggle with sufferings:"
—Hebrews 10: 32 (NKJV)

TODAY WE OFTEN SEE THE term, Flash, in technology. The Flash Player boasts of letting us effortlessly reach billions of people across browsers. Flashback is a term used particularly when the memory is recalled involuntarily.

Throughout the Book of Hebrews we receive flashbacks that provide a connection between the Old and New Testaments. These flashbacks effectively break down the message to provide clarity and enhance the vision for the future.

Like flashbacks, flashcards effectively break down key black letter law concepts. Here are some suggested ways to utilize flashcards:

- If you spend two hours writing criminal procedure practice essays, spend at least 30 minutes reviewing and memorizing flashcards on the same topic to solidify the rules of law.

- Review the MBE topic flashcards 30 minutes before your MBE session, then spend another two hours answering and reviewing 50 MBE.

- Spend the last two weeks before the exam using flashcards to review your more difficult subjects.

Now, let me see you give a big smile. Flash! Got it!

PRAYER:

"Dear Heavenly Father, thank you for your Son, Jesus Christ, who was sacrificed for my redemption to fulfill Your Will. Flashback: I am no longer at the mercy of animal sacrifices for my sins. Hallelujah! In Jesus' name, Amen."

SONG: "I Smile" by Kirk Franklin

"Getting to Best"

"He did evil because he had not set his heart on seeking the LORD."
—2 Chronicles 12:14 (NIV)

CHRONICLES FEATURES THE LIFE OF king Rehoboam where we get a lesson in privilege, pride and the judgment of God. One of the main problems with Rehoboam was that he simply refused to give God his absolute best. As a result, Rehoboam and his people paid a high price for his lack of clear direction and focus.

Are you giving your studies your best effort? Are you being honest with yourself? Perhaps there is time you could have used more efficiently, or managed better. Tell yourself each day that you will give it your best effort, offering no excuses. Everything that is done on a given day can be done better. Find ways of making those improvements by giving your best effort. Sometimes my child, pleased with a "B" grade, would be stunned when I simply asked, "Was this your best effort?"

Give your best in your bar studies, as you would in giving your best to God. He knows the desire of your heart, so be consistent in your pursuit. Work your studies wholeheartedly, giving it your very best. Getting to best entails no slacking, no ups and downs in commitment, no week on and week off in your schedule.

If we are not expecting the best from ourselves, we cannot expect the best from God.

Prayer:

"Dear Lord, teach me how to give my best to You, others, and self. In Jesus' name, Amen."

Song: "Give of Your Best to the Master"

DAY 22

"Got Power?"

"But to us there is but one God, the Father, of whom are all things,
and we in him; and one Lord Jesus Christ, by whom
are all things, and we by him."
—1Cor.8: 6 (KJV)

THE OTHER DAY I GRABBED my MAC laptop, placed it on my lap as I checked for updates to install. Proceeding to install one, the computer told me, "You are not connected to a power source." I certainly wasn't; I left my computer power cord lying in my office! But I couldn't update without the power source.

Today, I remind us, Jesus is the True power source. Lest we forget as we study day by day, hour by hour, minute by minute, that it is important to connect to the Almighty power source in all we do. Whisper a prayer of thanks or request for memory recall in between studies, or wherever fits your preference.

On the day of the bar exam, as you plug your laptop to the power source in the examining room, remember to simultaneously plug in to the Almighty power source.

Prayer:

"Almighty Father, there is none like you. Help me to always look to You as the source of my strength. In Jesus' name, Amen."

Song: "Just Wanna Say" by Israel Houghton

DAY 23

"The Key to Finishing Well"

"Let us run with endurance the race that God has set before us.
—Hebrews 12:1

EVERY CHRISTIAN IS ON A journey consecrated through Christ's sacrifice. The Apostle Paul calls the Christian life a race—a race that is a marathon, not a sprint. The race simply requires us to hold fast to our confession that Jesus Christ is our Lord and Savior, and to finish well. Endurance is the key to finishing well. Throughout the race of life we will have hills to climb, valleys to endure, detours, bumps, curves, rocky terrain, and stretches through the desert.

Perhaps you're at the point in your studies where you feel faint, and just plain tired. This is the time when you must exercise strict self-discipline. If you're well disciplined and committed to doing the practice MBE questions and essays under simulated test conditions, you're on the road to finishing well. Renew you spirit by remembering your purpose. Remain resilient. Persevere; there's a reward waiting.

PRAYER:

"Dear Heavenly Father, Give me the determination and perseverance to finish well for the Glory of God. In Jesus' Name, Amen."

SONG: "Walking" by Mary Mary

DAY 24

"Running on Empty?"

"Therefore we also, since we are surrounded by so great a cloud of witnesses, let us lay aside every weight, and the sin which so easily ensnares us, and let us run with endurance the race that is set before us, looking unto Jesus, the author and finisher of our faith, who for the joy that was set before Him endured the cross, despising the shame, and has sat down at the right hand of the throne of God. For consider Him who endured such hostility from sinners against Him, lest you become weary and discouraged in your souls."
—Hebrews 12: 1-3 (NKJV)

On Day 23 we stated that endurance is the key to finishing well. But, what drives endurance? Passion! The writer of Hebrews paints a vivid picture of people of faith who accomplished their missions because they were passionate about their purpose.

Here, the Hebrew writer causes us to think about the cloud of witnesses gone before us, then look at ourselves, and Jesus. Jesus ran His race with endurance, fixated on His passion to achieve our Father's purpose. Now, we have to run the race, watching out for potholes, bumps, and weights that encumber us as we seek to fulfill Christ's purpose.

In the race to the bar exam, it is easy to become encumbered with heavy weights: Working a job while studying, attending to family chores, emergencies, finances, poor time management, poor family support, doubt, and fear, to name a few. The fact of the matter is this: the bar exam is just an exam. Yes, there are significant consequences connected with the outcome; such as a job riding on your passing, but the consequences are not as looming as we make them out to be in our minds. You are already good at taking exams, or else you would not have made it this far. Be calm, keep your purpose in view, and endure this race by persisting with passion. A cloud of other law graduates have done it before you and succeeded. Now is your turn to get serious about finishing well.

PRAYER:

"Dear Heavenly Father, thank you for sending Your Son, Jesus, as the perfect example of endurance and finishing well. In Jesus' Name, Amen."

SONG: "The Father's Song" by Matt Redmon

"Passion leads to Purpose"

"Therefore we make it our aim, whether present or absent,
to be well pleasing to Him"
—2 Cor. 5:9 (NKJV)

THE KEY TO PASSION IS purpose. T. D. Jakes says, "If you can't figure out your purpose, figure out your passion. For your passion will lead you right into your purpose." We must run life's race with purpose, not aimlessly. We should direct our purpose toward pleasing God, even as it gives us a great sense of fulfillment. An ordinary cook gathers ingredients and mixes them according to the recipe, while a truly great chef throws her heart into the pot every time, and feels genuine, wrenching pain when the result is inadequate.

Do you feel strongly enough about becoming a Lawyer? Is this choice of a career your passion? If so, don't let anyone tell you that you cannot pass the bar exam. Not even you. At the end of the day, you simply need to remember to keep going. Daily renew your strength with prayer, passion, and purpose. Pick up your bar studies each day as a run with purpose fueled by vigor, passion, and determination to achieve your goal. When you finish well, sing your personal hallelujah song!

PRAYER:

"Dear Heavenly Father, thank you for creating me for Your purpose. In Jesus' Name, Amen."

SONG: "My Hallelujah Song" by Glorianne Hough

DAY 26

"There is No Competition"

"Do you not know that those who run in a race all run, but one receives the prize? Run in such a way that you may obtain it."
—1 Cor. 9:24-25 (NKJV)

In the Christian race we run with the intent to win the prize at the end of the race. Christ extends the offer to all of us. The good news is there's no competition; we can all win! Our prize is everlasting salvation as joint heirs in glory with Jesus Christ.

William van Horn, noted railway executive, quoted, "the biggest things are always the easiest to do because there is no competition." Like the Christian race, there is no competition in the race to the bar exam. Everybody can all win! It takes daily equipping yourself with rule of law memorizations, practice tests, essay writing, and efficiently and effectively using your resources. It also takes much prayer and supplication.

"If you want to become the best runner you can be, start now. Don't spend the rest of your life *wondering* if you can do it" (Priscilla Welch). After all, there's no competition.

PRAYER:

"Dear Heavenly Father, thank you for a new day with a renewed mind and attitude toward achieving my goals. In Jesus' Name, Amen."

SONG: "Amazing Grace" by Chris Tomlin

DAY 27

"No Regrets"

"Study to show thyself approved unto God, a workman who needeth not to be
ashamed, rightly dividing the word of truth."
—2 Timothy 2:15 (KJ21)

THE APOSTLE PAUL TELLS US that diligent Bible study leads to approval from God. God expects us to familiarize ourselves with His Word. By studying God's Word, shamelessly, we learn how to live, lead, and receive directions to salvation. With the knowledge that we are doing what God expects of us, studying His Word becomes fulfilling and satisfying.

As an aspirant for licensing in the discipline of Law, you must faithfully study to show yourself approved, so that when you look back over what you did in preparation, you will not be ashamed. There will be no regrets. When giving helpful tips for passing the bar exam, a former bar examiner in California said, ". . . the only way that you are going to pass the bar exam is if you spend enough time learning bar exam law and practicing bar exam questions." Be strong and experience NO lack of resolve in performing your bar exam studies, just as the apostle Paul admonishes us to study the Word of God.

PRAYER:

"Dear Lord, Help me to remain grounded in Your Word. Also, please help me remain grounded in my bar studies. Thank you, Father. In Jesus' Name, Amen."

SONG: "Me Without You" by TobyMac

DAY 28

"Do You, too"

"But Jesus often withdrew to lonely places and prayed."
—Luke 5:16 (NIV)

WHILE IT MAY SEEM IRRELEVANT and a distraction, you must keep your body healthy while studying for the bar exam. Physical activity helps during this marathon. There is a tendency to neglect our health when under pressure, or during stressful times. Fit your personal health and sanity in your plan—at least 30 minutes of "do you" time. Maintain good sleep, eating, exercise, and prayer habits. Take breaks in between study sessions. Learn some stretching techniques that relieve tension.

It was Jesus' custom to take care of Himself by withdrawing from the crowds to be alone and pray. His example teaches us that sometimes we must break away from our hectic schedules and refresh ourselves so that we can be more successful in our work. Prayer gives us renewed spiritual power and sanity from God. Exercise, sleep, and good eating habits give us strength and energy. So, do you, when you get the opportunity.

Prayer:

"Dear Lord, I pray for bar examiners as I pray for myself. Help them be wise in their administration and exercise of their responsibility. May I be wise enough to get proper rest during my bar studies so that I will have my thoughts organized. In Jesus' name, Amen."

Song: "Tis So Sweet" by Casting Crowns

DAY 29

"The Trust Agreement"

"But He knows the way that I take; when He has
tested me, I will come forth as gold."
—Job 23:10 (NIV)

HENRY KISSINGER ONCE SAID "A diamond is merely a lump of coal that did well under pressure." To successfully perform under pressure is to stay well while staying challenged. Job is one of the best examples of perseverance, endurance, and thriving under pressure recorded in the Old Testament. Here, when Job speaks of the way that he takes, he is speaking of the furtherance and conduct of his life. Therefore, Job gives his life away. Job, as settlor, entrusts his life to God. I can imagine Job, with strong intent, resolved, "I (trustee/settlor) give my entire life (trust property) to God. I require God (the Trustee) to care for me (the beneficiary), and make such gift and provision for me as required for my support." Job helps us understand how we can experience life under pressure and circumstances that seem to dictate doom.

You are at least four or five weeks from the last week before the bar exam. Your schedule has been filled with bar review course lectures, MBE practice tests and reviews, essay practice tests and reviews, memorizations, flashcards, and more. Some of you are truly enjoying it, some are coping well, and some are beginning to feel the pressures. If that person is you, give it away! Entrust it to God. Go back and read DAY FOUR's inspirational moment for refreshing.

Diligently prepare to take your test and come forth as pure gold.

PRAYER:

"O Lord, pressures surmount but I have belief, faith and trust in You. In Jesus' Name, Amen."

SONG: "Gold" By Nicole Britt

DAY 30

"Encouraging One"

"Therefore, encourage each other with these words."
—1 Thessalonians 4:18 (NIV)

THE OTHER DAY I CAME across an encouraging note written in beautiful hand script to my daughter from one of her classmates/friends while in high school over eight years ago:

> *"Hey, this is a note of encouragement,"* the writer says. *"I know u don't feel well but keep ya head up Hun; I hope u feel better later. Do good in school 2 because it's beginning to become stressful. Trust me I know!"* She continues, *"But we almost done so keep the good head on your shoulders! Be easy and enjoy this week, ok? Becuz I can't have my friend sick and then stressin' 2. I need u at school."*

Encouraging words make a difference. They can make people feel good about themselves; causing them to want to step out to reach their dreams. God wants us to be the kind of person who speaks words of encouragement and praise that build others up according to their needs (Ephesians 4:29).

Take time out to encourage a fellow bar exam student when the opportunity arises. In doing so you please God, and will feel good about stepping outside your own pressures. That high school student summed it best when she said, "but we're almost done, so keep the good head on your shoulders!"

You are almost done with your bar studies. The race is nearing its end. Stay encouraged and encourage someone else.

PRAYER:

"Almighty Father, sometimes it takes an innocent child or youth to teach us some simple lesson in Christian principles. Help me to speak encouraging words daily to others and myself. In Jesus' Name, Amen."

SONG: "I Need You, You Need Me" by Hezekiah Walker

DAY 31

"Follow Your Examples of Faith"

"Now faith is the substance of things hoped for, the evidence of things not seen. For by it the elders obtained a good testimony."
—Hebrews 11:1-2 (KJV)

IMAGINE HOW YOUR ANCESTORS LIVED. Take a minute and reflect on your grandparents, or their parents. Did your ancestors manage to overcome a myriad of personal and societal problems, such as severe illnesses, wars, inequities, loss of loved ones or severe economic declines? Did any of them succeed against the odds? Compared to their societal struggles, world wars, and great depressions, a bar exam should be a breeze! Sometimes we have to reflect on past struggles and achievements to muster the strength to pick up the baton and run an extra mile with faith.

Here, in Hebrews 11, the chapter called the "Hall of Faith," the apostle Paul takes his audience back to memories of past ancestors, men and women of faith, who triumphed in their own lifetimes. The reflections served to glorify God and help the Hebrew people understand perseverance, vision, sacrifice, and passion.

By now you may be struggling with the demands of bar exam studies, wishing you could have a week to "chill," or just stop juggling between tasks. The truth of the matter is, there are far greater struggles in life, and you are standing on the shoulders of ancestors who endured so much more.

PRAYER:

"Dear Heavenly Father, I know that without faith it is impossible to please You. Please help me develop a trusting relationship with you. In Jesus' name, Amen."

SONG: "Faith of Our Fathers" by the Mormon Tabernacle Choir

DAY 32

"Second Wind"

"But those who hope in the LORD will renew their strength. They will soar on wings like eagles; they will run and not grow weary, they will walk and not be faint."
—Isaiah 40:31 (NIV)

"Second wind" is a phenomenon in distance running whereby an athlete who is too out of breath and tired to continue suddenly finds the strength to press on at top performance with less exertion. The feeling may be similar to that of a "runner's high", the most obvious difference being that the runner's high occurs after the race is over.

As the bar exam study draws to an end, some of you may be experiencing weariness and fatigue. Some of you, unfortunately, may be working full-time jobs and studying for the bar exam. The dual roles may have stretched you. Many of you have been faithful in following your bar study schedule; attending your bar course review lectures on site or online; diligently working practice tests and essays; daily praising God. Yet now, you are breathless and in need of a second wind.

If you are in need of renewal, your "second wind", look up and put your trust in God. There is nothing wrong with praying for strength. Just as an athlete needs the proper training and discipline to keep fit for the race, we, as Christians, also need to keep in spiritual shape in order to run the race God has set before us.

PRAYER:

"Heavenly Father, thank you for strength to endure life's circumstances. I am studying for my bar exam and getting weary. Give me renewal of body, mind, and strength. Revive me with a second wind so I can complete and win my race. In Jesus' Name, Amen"

SONG: "I'll praise you in this storm" by Casting Crowns

DAY 33

"Single Focus"

"Brethren, I count not myself to have apprehended: but this one thing I do,
forgetting those things which are behind, and reaching forth unto those things
which are before, I press toward the mark for the
prize of the high calling of God in Christ Jesus."
—Philippians 3:13-14 (KJV)

THE APOSTLE PAUL HAD A singleness and focus of purpose. Paul summed up his life with the words, "for me to live is Christ." Absolutely nothing could separate or distract Paul from his purpose. He put all past things behind and focused on pressing toward the mark!

Adopt Paul's fortitude as you press toward the mark in your bar exam studies. If you did not pass a previous exam:

> (a). Put past failures behind you. It's a new day. You are preparing for your fresh anointing.

(b). Forget negative comments from those Nay-Sayers. I remember a "well-wishing" neighbor saying to me, "Honey, maybe God wants you to pursue a different direction. Sometimes you just have to move on." And move on is what I did—straight off her grounds, putting her naysaying words behind me. I was strong enough in my conviction and faith to know God's purpose for me and the promises He made.

(c). Continue to pray and study God's Word as you study for the bar exam. In prayer, speak to God like speaking to a friend. Give God your fears, worries, and receive strength and direction.

With a determined resolve, reach for the prize. Run with certainty, and do not waver. You should have your "second wind" by now, just in time to take your first simulated bar exam on this marathon. Take deep breaths, remember those ancestors who endured far greater tests, look up, whisper a prayer, and go forth. Your prize is just ahead.

PRAYER:

"Dear Best Friend, thanks for believing in me, as I in you. Help me to shake off all things that take my eyes off you. Help me to shake off thoughts and negative comments that impede achieving my purpose. In Jesus' Name, Amen."

SONG: "My God is Awesome" by Charles Jenkins

DAY 34

"Are You Listening, Or Drifting?"

"For this reason we must pay much closer attention to what
we have heard, lest we drift away from it."
—Hebrews 2:1 (RKJV)

LIKE LEAKY VESSELS, WITHOUT GREAT care, our minds and memories do not always retain what it receives. It is as if we did not listen. The word, listen, in Scripture simply means to focus and concentrate and to pay attention by opening our ears to hear. When we listen, we open our minds and hearts to God's Truth. We will also hear what godly people are saying that will sharpen and help us.

Listening creates an effective relationship between God and us. The mature Christian cannot grow in maturity unless he or she listens to God's Word. Temptations, worldly cares, fears, and pleasures may cause our minds and memories to drift. Drifting is not an option. God expects us to listen and follow His Word.

Likewise, drifting is not an option as you intensify your bar exam studies for the next few weeks. Actively listen to the lectures to maximize retention and control drifting. Set aside all other thoughts and behaviors and concentrate on the message.

PRAYER:

"Dear Heavenly Father, remove my drifting tendencies. Help me to become a better listener of Your Truth. Bless me with knowledge retention and recall for the bar exam. Thank you, and In Jesus' name, Amen."

SONG: "God Speaking" by Mandisa

DAY 35

"Power Outage"

"Now to him who is able to do immeasurably more than all we ask or imagine, according to his power that is at work within us,"
—Ephesians 3:20

ARNOLD PALMER, RENOWNED GOLFER, RECALLS a lesson about overconfidence during the 1961 Masters tournament when he had a one-stroke lead and had just hit a great tee shot. Palmer felt he was in pretty good shape. Seeing an old friend standing at the edge at the gallery, Arnold, after receiving a motion from the old friend, went to greet the friend and shake his hand. Arnold recalls that at the moment he left the game to shake the friend's hand, he knew he had lost his focus. Says Arnold Palmer, *"I missed a putt and lost the Masters. You don't forget a mistake like that; you just learn from it and become more determined that you will never do it again."*

The score was 28 to 6. Then, the lights went out. During the 2013 Super Bowl game in New Orleans the power in the Super—dome went out for 34 minutes. For 34 minutes the players had to sit and wait for the power source. The news announcer said the players were told by their coaches to stay on the field and wait it out while stretching so they wouldn't lose focus. Losing focus was the biggest challenge for the teams those long 34 minutes. Sure enough, when the game resumed, the winning team's momentum had been compromised to the point of winning the Super Bowl by only a field goal margin!

Take care not to experience "power outage" and loss of focus on your journey to the bar exam. Our Scripture today is the conclusion of the Apostle's prayer, in which the POWER of God is celebrated. God's power is like the Long Arm Statute that reaches all things, everybody. His power and authority is actual, apparent, and ratified! Further, God's power is absolute, and to all things that have been, or shall be, and to things impossible with us. He can do above all that we ask or think. Stay plugged in to His power source. Stay focused on Him and trust His guidance as you also stay focused in your bar exam studies.

Prayer:

"Dear Powerful, Almighty God, thank you for your mercy. I praise You, the One from whom all blessings flow. In Jesus' name, Amen."

Song: "Hold On to the Promises" by Sanctus Real

"Hone In"

"If the axe is dull and its edge unsharpened, more strength is needed but skill will bring success."
—Ecclesiastes 10:10

To HONE IN ON SOMETHING is to give it all your attention, thereby sharpening or perfecting that "something." An example of honing in is a basketball player perfecting her free throw before a big game. Often we see people whose "axes" are dull, but working harder than others; yet, they are not as successful. It takes them a longer time to get to where they want to be. However, those with "sharpened axes" accomplish more and with a far better quality than those with dull "axes." The same is true regarding our faith: A sharpened faith reaps a better reward.

We are created for a purpose. God wants people who are honed in to fulfill their purpose, and who refuse to grow weary even when fainting and giving way to exhaustion are justifiable.

While it may appear like a looming beast in a corner, the bar exam is really one of the greatest learning opportunities. It's a time to really release all that you have painstakingly studied, display your analytical thinking, time management skills, and faith. Hone in and You Can Do this! Be faithful in your meditation and studies, do not drift, do not cheat yourself, and God will provide strength to the end.

PRAYER:

"Thank you, Lord, for honing me through my reading of Your Scriptures. Lord, I pray for the ability to continue to hone my skills in legal studies. May my sharpened knowledge and skills in law be used to glorify You. In Jesus' name, Amen."

SONG: "Strong Enough" by Matthew West

DAY 37

"Peripheral Vision"

"And Peter answered him and said, Lord, if it be thou, bid me come unto thee on the water. And he said, Come. And when Peter was come down out of the ship, he walked on the water, to go to Jesus. But when he saw the wind boisterous, he was afraid; and beginning to sink, he cried, saying, Lord, save me. And immediately Jesus stretched forth his hand, and caught him, and said unto him, O thou of little faith, wherefore didst thou doubt?"
—Matthew 14:28-31 (KJV)

PERIPHERAL VISION IS SIDE VISION, a part of vision that occurs outside the very center of gaze. When you FOCUS on something, peripheral vision is blurred. Sometimes we allow things in our peripheral vision to distract us on our journey, or even change our course.

In our Scripture lesson, Peter was walking on the water, focusing on Jesus. When Peter engaged his peripheral vision, took his eyes off Jesus, he began to concentrate on the storm. Changing the focus to his fears, Peter began sinking. Peter let fear shift the focus from Jesus.

Do not allow the thought of potential difficulties with the bar exam blind you to God's power to help and His promise to guide through this journey. Keep your peripheral vision blurred.

PRAYER:

"Dear Most High God, thank you for being all powerful, loving, and forgiving. May I always see You as my strength in the midst of every storm, trial, challenge, or tribulation. In Jesus' name, Amen."

SONG: "Open My Eyes That I May See"

DAY 38

"Rest well"

"And he said to them, Come away by yourselves to a desolate place and rest a while. For many were coming and going, and they had no leisure even to eat."

—Mark 6:31

ONE OF ENGLAND'S BEST KNOWN preachers, C.H. Surgeon, quoted, *"rest time is not waste time."*—We are expected to get at least eight hours of restful sleep every night. Sleep is important for natural development of melatonin, a hormone secreted by a gland in the brain which helps regulate other hormones and maintains the body's rhythm. When it is dark, the body produces more melatonin; hence it's nickname, the "hormone of darkness."

Issue in today's Scripture: Jesus' disciples have been on a mission surrounded by crowds, preaching, working miracles, and walking for an extensive period of time. The Disciples return to Jesus visibly tired and fatigued.

Jesus' Words/Rule: Under Mark's scripture 6:31, Jesus Said, "Come with me by yourselves to a quiet place and get some rest."

Analysis: Here, Jesus did not look at them and say, "Let's keep going. Pick up an Energy Drink!" Instead, Jesus compassionately offers Himself, a quiet place, and rest.

Conclusion: Therefore, rest is downright biblical. Jesus emphasizes the need for us to rest and take the time to sharpen or refresh ourselves.

During the few weeks before the bar exam, your sleep habits and nutrition are key. The intense nature of the bar exams requires a person to be well rested and alert. If you find yourself angry, tired, or weak today, the answer may *not* be another study book, workout session, or more lectures for the bar exam. The answer may not be more of ANYTHING. The answer may be Jesus, quiet place, and rest.

Prayer:

"Dear Heavenly Father, thank you for teaching me the importance of rest. Help me to answer my body's call for rest. In Jesus' name, Amen."

Song: "Rest in Me" by Todd Vaters

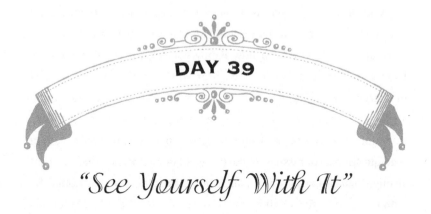

DAY 39

"See Yourself With It"

"May He give you the desire of your heart and
make all your plans succeed."
—Psalm 20:4

I ENCOUNTERED A MAJOR ROADBLOCK AND detour one morning while traveling from my home city to work in a city 110 minutes away. The detour took me an additional 40 minutes in a roundabout way to reach my destination. I was facing unfamiliar roadways under inclement weather conditions, but I faithfully prayed and kept my map (GPS) in view in order to reach my destination on this new course.

See yourself with it. Fix your mind on where you want to be in life. Set your goal. Map it. Keep it in view; then, diligently plan, and execute your journey to attain it. There may be some bumps and roadblocks on the journey; but, like the windshield in your car, you can still see your destination ahead despite the bumps, minor accidents, and roadblocks.

When problems arrive, seek the Word on it, and proclaim the Word even when you don't see it, and watch things change.

Can you see yourself as an attorney? Recapture your feeling the day you graduated from Law School after three grueling years of hard work and focus. Think on how happy you felt to receive your Jurist Doctor degree, and to add "J.D." after your name! Now, see yourself in a large center, sitting on the floor, leaning on a wall, or standing in a group, or sitting in a bathroom stall, whispering a prayer of thanks, surrounded by the buzz of hundreds of applicants anxiously ready to read questions, spot issues, impart rule of law, and write great, relevant, strong, logical analyses and conclusions! Imagine yourself doing that with calm, collective confidence. Next, see yourself standing before the Supreme Court judges, lifting your right hand to swear in oath to uphold the laws of your state Bar. Feel your pride and see your tears of joy. See yourself quietly whispering a prayer of thanks.

Now, see you, the Lawyer. Envision yourself greeting a potential client, handing your card, and saying, "Hello, I am Attorney—, and I'm pleased to meet you," while silently whispering a prayer of thanks. Now, make your imaginations a reality. Forge ahead in your studies.

Prayer:

"Dear Heavenly Father, please grant my goal and send miraculous blessings to me for passing the Bar exam and becoming an attorney. Thank you for good thoughts and positive energy. I give You all the honor, glory, and praise, for showing me Your favor. In Jesus' name, Amen."

Song: "Imagine Me" by Kirk Franklin

DAY 40

"Feedback"

"Poverty and disgrace are for the one who ignores instruction,
but one who heeds reproof is honored."
—Proverbs 13:18

THE MERE MENTION OF THE words, "performance review," visibly changes an employee's composure, in many instances. Sometimes I dreaded this ritual. Why? Because, for many, the art of giving and receiving feedback, which should occur throughout the year, is a "springing" annual event of dumping comments and observations about performance previously unaware by the employee.

Proverbs 13:18, with its simple, moral illustration, highlight and teach a fundamental reality about feedback for us to contemplate. First, the person who is so proud that he scorns or refuses good feedback or instruction, as if it is a reflection on his honor, liberty, or own knowledge, is despised as foolish, stubborn, and ungovernable. Second, the one who humbly accepts feedback and instruction will follow through by ameliorating what is awry when it is shown to her. That person gains respect and proves herself to be wise and honorable.

Grading feedback during your bar studies is important. Having each practice test personally graded is quite helpful in measuring your bar exam readiness. Graded feedback from my bar review course essay writing tutor proved invaluable! He was very constructively critical in his electronic highlighted comments. Asking me pointed questions while explaining why an analysis was incomplete; giving me low points to make me work harder was a blessing.

Having detailed feedback with both positive and negative comments will be a big factor in your success.

PRAYER:

"Dear Heavenly Father, please give me the strength that I need to face today and continued bar exam studies. I am not worried about tomorrow; just give me the strength that I need today. And, Lord, please give me a receptive heart and mind to receive constructive feedback. In Jesus' name, Amen."

SONG: "Lose My Soul" by Tobymac

DAY 41

"The Fear Factor"

"Then the man who had received one bag of gold came. 'Master,' he said, 'I knew that you are a hard man, harvesting where you have not sown and gathering where you have not scattered seed. So I was afraid and went out and hid your gold in the ground. See, here is what belongs to you."
—Matthew 25:24-26 (NIV)

NOTICE WHAT THE PARABLE SAYS about the man with the one bag of gold: He was afraid and went and hid the gold in the ground. In his fear of failure the foolish servant laid aside the one bag and gained nothing more, no interest. He was afraid he wouldn't be a good enough steward over his small blessing. God tells us not to have such fear.

The bar exam is a couple of weeks away. This is not the time to become restrained by the fear of failure. Free yourself to welcome the bar challenges knowing you gave the studies your very best effort. Are you confident that you were a good, faithful steward in your studies? Can you truthfully say, "no regrets?" Are you honing in on your skills during this final stretch? Then, be careful not to succumb to the restraints of fear.

It happens even to animals. After a circus performance, two elephants were being tied: The mother elephant was tied loosely to a small stake with a thin rope, while the baby elephant was tied tightly to a strong stake with a thick rope. When asked why the trainer tied the baby elephant more tightly than the mother elephant, the tamer said, "*The baby elephant is not fully trained and gives her very best energy trying to pull the stake out of the ground to which it is tied and run free. That is why I tie the baby elephant to a heavy stake with a thick rope. However, the mother elephant remembers that in her babyhood she tried repeatedly to get away but couldn't. So the mother elephant doesn't even TRY to escape once she notices that she is chained. That's why I can tie the mother elephant to a little stake.*"

Here, The fear of failure stopped the mother elephant from running free. The mother elephant possessed the physical and inner strength to break free from that little stake, but she didn't **believe** she could. She had the breakthrough power, but, instead, gave her power to Fear.

Moreover, the mother elephant lets the memory of past failures keep her from believing she could ever free herself from the rope, so she gives up based on the past.

You are almost at the end of this race to the bar exam. Believe you can succeed, claim your breakthrough, release past failures, and make God's Power yours.

Thomas Edison summed it with this quote, "Many of life's failures are people who did not realize how close they were to success when they gave up."

PRAYER:

"God, our Father, help me relax and prepare to welcome the bar exam with open arms, just as I welcome you. Lord, I know every facet of my life belongs to you. Give me the strength to trust, believe, and succeed. In Jesus' name, Amen."

SONG: "Hold On" by Tobymac

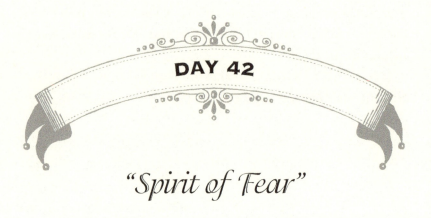

DAY 42

"Spirit of Fear"

"Peace I leave with you; my peace I give you. I do not give to you as the world gives. Do not let your hearts be troubled and do not be afraid."
—John 14:27

THE "SPIRIT OF FEAR" KEEPS us from being cogent Christians or happy people by using our own fears. It links with worry and causes misery. Fear makes us skeptical, short-sighted, and selfish (afraid to commit to God, others, ourselves). Worst, fear kills faith!

Fear kills movement and faith keeps movement. Decide *now* to tame your fear and step forward in faith!

PRAYER:

"Heavenly Father, Your Word says let not my heart be troubled, neither let it be afraid. Father, I come to You because I need to cast my worries, my fears, and cares upon You. Your Word says that I can because You care for me. So Father, I cast all my cares, all my worries, all my anxieties, all my problems, all my doubts, all my fears, and all of my needs concerning this bar exam upon You. In Jesus' Name. A-men."

SONG: "Have Faith in God" by Hillsong

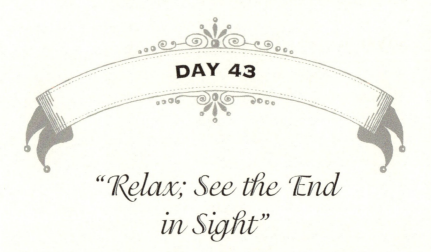

"Relax; See the End in Sight"

"Do not be anxious about anything, but in every situation, by prayer and petition, with thanksgiving, present your requests to God."
—Philippians 4:6

THE BEST PART ABOUT THE home stretch on your race, these last two weeks before the bar exam, is that you are close enough to see it all start coming together, but far enough away to still be learning.

Sometimes seeing the end in sight brings on anxiety. The stretch has been mentally challenging and overwhelming. You may even feel you are running out of time. Don't give in to the anxiety. If a day or two off will recharge you, take them, and resume re-energized!

All of us experience anxiety at times; it's human nature. Anxiety, worry and tension occur when we face a situation and choose to rely upon our own strength rather than upon God and His Word. Replacing anxiety with prayer and thanksgiving brings peace of mind.

Do not belittle your capabilities. Relax; the end is in sight. Besides, you're running with the King!

PRAYER:

"Lord, I'm running for my prize, and I won't stop now. Thank you for continued strength and endurance. In Jesus' name, Amen."

SONG: "I Can See Clearly Now" By Jimmy Cliff

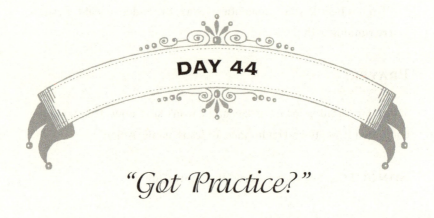

DAY 44

"Got Practice?"

"But be doers of the word, and not hearers only, deceiving yourselves."
—James 1:22

OUR MAIN PURPOSE IN READING and studying the Scriptures should be to receive God's instructions for practical application. We study to practice. James, in our Scripture, tells us to be practitioners of the Word, rather than mere recipients of His knowledge.

A person who wants to win a bicycling race could study all aspects of traditional training plans, but the real performance comes from practice. Becoming highly knowledgeable on the subject is useless if it's not put into practice for good performance.

The same is true for bar exam studies. There must be diligent practice in order to perform well on the bar exam. Study from your mistakes on MBE practice questions and compare your essays with sample essays provided by your bar review course. Read outlines once, then put them aside and start practicing.

When approaching the end, practice testing should be the primary training for the home stretch. Do not worry that you do not have a clue as to what the law is in a certain area. Identify the issues and check your work later. The attitude that you do not know the law well enough to write an essay on a given subject is negative thinking. Write your practice essay and check it against the bar review course. The few days you have remaining to PRACTICE are vital toward your success. Do not become a slacker this close to the finish line.

Studying for the bar exam can be monotonous, frustrating, tiring, all-consuming, and certainly not fun. But you didn't get this far in the race to fall two laps behind. The optimum word to finishing well is "practice." If you have difficulty keeping that word in focus, remember attorneys PRACTICE law.

PRAYER:

"Heavenly Father, I am grateful for Your endurance and encouragement; I hunger for both. Thank you for granting me Your favor. In Jesus' name, Amen."

SONG: "Believe" by Brooks and Dunn

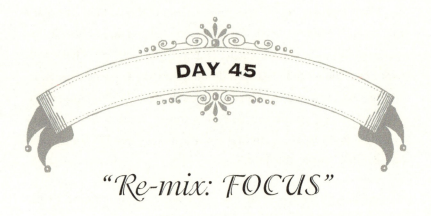

"Re-mix: FOCUS"

"Finally, brothers, whatever is true, whatever is noble, whatever is right, whatever is pure, whatever is lovely, whatever is admirable—if anything is excellent or praiseworthy—think about such things."
—Philippians 4:8

LET'S REVISIT THE SUBJECT OF focus. There are times during a race when the runner's fatigue seems mind-boggling and thoughts turn contrary. This is the point at which total focus on running the race becomes eminent. The runner no longer thinks about the aching muscles, tightening chest, or burning feet. The mind becomes totally transfixed by the process of running in a smooth and coordinated way, with no worry about the speed, the distance from the finish line, or how soon is the next Gatorade stop. The runner becomes completely immersed in the run, with no distracting thoughts or doubts.

The race to the bar exam can become a mentally transfixing experience, too. Start by releasing unproductive exam anxiety, and put your thoughts on the Excellency that surrounds Christ and all things good. While a little anxiety can be a good thing because it keeps us motivated and alert, too much anxiety may be crippling. Let's face it, despite our best motivational and inspirational efforts, fear may creep in. Be prepared to discard that spirit of fear with prayer, extreme focus, and give the bar exam your very best effort.

The scripture, above, exhorts us to focus on good thoughts and excellence. There is no excellence in fear, other than the fear of God. We are encouraged to bring our thoughts into submission to Jesus Christ by learning to think biblically about every aspect of life. Our thoughts are real and powerful, even though they cannot be seen, weighed, or measured. Quite frankly, our thoughts mold our actions. Warren Wiersbe, in his commentary, says,

> *"Sow a thought, reap an action.*
> *Sow an action, reap a habit.*
> *Sow a habit, reap a character.*
> *Sow a character, reap a destiny!"*

(Wiersbe, W. W., 1986, c1989. The Bible exposition commentary. "An exposition of the New Testament comprising the entire 'BE' series"—Jkt. (Php 4:8). Wheaton, Ill.: Victor Books)

What are your thoughts about reaching your goal of becoming an attorney? Do your actions reflect your focus on those thoughts? Are you back on track, refreshed and ready to become mentally transfixed on the run (your studies), ever giving praise to Him from whom all blessings flow? Just a few more laps/tracks to go.

PRAYER:

"Dear Heavenly Father, I just need to be able to focus. I need your help to look at this information so I can remember and apply it well on my bar exam. Please help me feel more confident going into the test and relax a bit so I can concentrate. Heavenly Father, please help my family and friends to understand that I need to focus and study. In Jesus' name, Amen."

SONG: "Blessed Assurance, Jesus is Mine" by Fannie J. Crosby

 DAY 46

"A Made Up Mind"

"So humble yourselves before God.
Resist the devil, and he will flee from you."
—James 4:7 (NLT)

"Jesus said to him, 'Away from me, Satan! For it is written:
'Worship the Lord your God, and serve him only.'"
—Matthew 4:10

As a child, our daughter could be obstinately unmoving when she believed, as a four-year-old, that her way was the best course of action. Consequently, she would go to daycare with the matching top to one outfit and matching bottom to another, or a white sock on one foot and blue on another, quite pleased with her decision. Without a doubt, she had her mind made up; she was stubborn!

A "made up mind" tenacity is advantageous in certain circumstances; such as, a made up mind to pass the bar. The bar student needs a mind that is fixed or set in purpose with a resolve obstinately maintained that he will pass the bar exam. But it will not work if you are not properly preparing, and strong enough in your resolve to resist temptations.

In the Bible, the Devil appears, most famously, as Job's tormentor and Jesus' tempter. Both rebuked Satan with a made up mind to follow their courses of action, which led to obeying God's will. A made up mind is likely to be tested as you prepare for the bar exam. How? Fear, which we have learned is not a spirit of God, may creep in. Anxiety may quietly lift its head bringing physical symptoms. When they slowly emerge, nip them in the bud as Jesus and Job did: With prayer, scripture, and obstinacy. Turn to Psalms 46 and 91, and John 14 as suggested readings.

Your tedious studying will soon come to an end. Until then, have a made up mind to pass.

PRAYER:

"Dear Heavenly Father, I fear no evil for You are with me. I place my trust in You for my safety and guidance. You are my God and my judge. You are the one I seek to please and honor. My strength is in you. In Jesus' name, Amen."

SONG: "Gotta A Made Up Mind" by Hasan Green

DAY 47

"God's Favor"

"May our Lord Jesus Christ himself and God our Father, who loved us and by his grace gave us eternal encouragement and good hope, encourage your hearts and strengthen you in every good deed and word."
—2 Thessalonians 2:16-17

GOD'S FAVOR IS ABOUT GOD being with us in the midst of our struggles, joys, and quest to fulfill our dreams. Joel Osteen, Senior Pastor of the largest church in America, describes God's Favor by saying, "I believe God's favor is something intangible where you've got God's blessings on your lives. I'm not saying it's not a struggle, but you believe for good things."

Every Christian should desire and seek God's Favor. Believe you are entitled to a passing score on the bar exam; believe you have the ability, favor, and CAN pass. Be confident in your knowledge of the law. Continue to practice, practice, and practice. You have clients coming to you in a few days during the bar exam. Believe you can spot their legal issues among all the irrelevant information, breakdown the issues into their compound rules and elements, apply the clients' facts to the rules and elements, and quickly apply sound legal reasoning and analysis between facts, rules, and elements to properly advise your client.

Yes, you CAN pass the bar exam.

Prayer:

"Dear Heavenly Father, I pray for Your favor, and that I will pass the bar exam that I take in a few days. I know the Law, Lord. Thank you for your favor. In Jesus' name, Amen."

Song: "God' s Favor" by Sharon Clark Sheard, Kelly Price, Donald Lawrence, and Kim Burrell

DAY 48

"You Don't Know What You Don't Know, or Do You?"

"That is why we never give up. Though our bodies are dying, our spirits are being renewed every day."
—2 Corinthians 4:16

PASSING THE BAR EXAM ISN'T just about memorizing the law. It is about practicing and applying the law. It is about memorizing the black letter law rules so you can clearly and concisely write them down on an essay answer.

Accept the fact that it is literally impossible to know everything that could possibly be tested on the Bar exam. Be mentally prepared to see an essay problem where you don't know the rule of law. What do you do? You use logical legal reasoning and analysis, make up a rule, apply the facts, and write like a lawyer advising the client. Keep it simple, lest you really show the examiners you don't know what you don't know. Most bar exam essay examiners only spend a few minutes reading essay answers, so write clearly, succinctly, and simply. Even Jesus kept it simple when he taught using parables: Clear, simple messages giving story facts then applying His rule and conclusion for Christian living.

Persistence is the key to forging on when you don't know what you don't know, but you do know enough legal reasoning to make up your own rule. The Bible tells us that those who endure to the end will be saved (Matthew 24:13). The temptation to quit in anything is especially strong when our feelings and our body run out of energy. But those who pray and depend on God are renewed in their spirit. Whatever you do, don't quit! Answer every essay question.

PRAYER:

"Dear Almighty God, if I go by my feelings when I face an unknown, I may give up. Fear, anxiety, and doubt, wage a strong battle inside me. Thank you for giving me your strength so I will persist. In Jesus' name, Amen."

SONG: "What A Friend We Have In Jesus" by Oakridge Boys

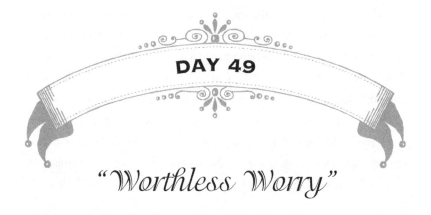

DAY 49

"Worthless Worry"

"For I am about to do a brand-new thing.
See, I have already begun! Do you not see it?"
—Isaiah 43:19a (NLT)

WORRY IS WASTING TODAY'S TIME to mess up tomorrow's opportunities with yesterday's troubles. While you make the best laid plans for your final week of bar studies, life happens. It's called Murphy's Law, an adage that typically states, "Anything that can go wrong will go wrong." Maybe a family member gets very sick, the job has a top priority action that requires you to be there rather than studying, you have to suddenly travel out-of-town, you get sick or hurt, or the computer you plan to use for the bar exam suddenly crashes. Worry and frustration seeps in. Then, there are those who will worry about what could go wrong before anything ever happens. After all, it's your LAST week! Something simply has to go wrong, right? Wrong. But life happens. The way you handle what life brings on your final lap in this race to the bar exam depends largely on your attitude and discernment.

As a Reserve Soldier for many years, I became indoctrinated in safety precautions and warnings to the point of frustration for my husband as I constantly check the security of our home. I consider it smart; he considers it worry about nothing. One day I read the story of a woman who had been having trouble getting to sleep at night because she feared burglars. One night her husband heard a noise in the house, so he went downstairs to investigate. When he got there, he did, indeed, find a burglar. "Good evening," said the man of the house. "I am pleased to see you. Come upstairs and meet my wife. She has been waiting 10 years to meet you." (William Marshall, Eternity Shut in a Span.) Worry drains our strength and produces self-induced burdens. It does not make us escape the baneful, but it does make us ill-suited to cope with it when it comes.

God is working a "new thing" in your life. Can't you see it? Do not waste time and energy with worry. Continue to practice MBE questions, write essays, memorize, and pray so you can see the new things God wants to work in your life. Get plenty of rest, establish a good sleep routine for the bar exam days ahead, and depend on God.

PRAYER:

"Dear Heavenly Father, thank you for the blessings you have placed in my life. Thank you for being with me during my bar exam studies when I feel a bit overwhelmed. Thank you for always being there and allowing me to rely on you. I praise you. In Jesus' name, Amen."

SONG: "Need you Now" by Plumb

DAY 50

Final Weekend Before Bar Exam

DAY ONE

"True North"

"and he sent a man before them—Joseph, sold as a slave. They bruised his feet with shackles, his neck was put in irons, till what he foretold came to pass, till the word of the Lord proved him true."
—Psalm 105:17-19

DURING MY OFFICER TRAINING AS a Soldier, I had to become proficient in map reading, terrains, and navigation skills. I learned that following the compass needle to get True North would not work. True North is a constant and refers to the geographic North Pole. The compass gives magnetic north, which tends to shift and refers to the pole of the Earth's magnetic field. Maps are aligned along True North, so I had to make adjustments when navigating by compass.

God is our True North. He is constant, never shifting. We, however, shift. One moment we trust Him to lead and guide us through the bar exam; next, we succumb to fear, doubt, worry, and anxiety. That is normal, for it identifies our human nature. But we should quickly re-navigate ourselves, and make adjustments to get our "compass" realigned along True North.

Through all the problems that Joseph faced, he stood fast to the true constant, almighty God, to deliver him from the struggles. God was preparing and building Joseph as he aligned him on the path for greatness. God is always doing great things in our lives even when we are engulfed with struggles. He gages our compass, measuring our growth. God is far more concerned about how we conduct ourselves in the face of our struggles than the struggles we face.

Face the bar exam boldly, confidently and dare yourself not to fail! You studied smart and diligently enough to make that declaration. Align your map (goal) along the True North (God, the constant), navigate ahead and claim your victory. You are going to pass this exam.

Prayer:

"Dear Lord, True North of my life, giver of all good gifts, enter into my mind and heart. Please give me the gift of knowledge and the grace to use it wisely. Give me perseverance and fortitude. Help my memory, that I may remember what I learn and recall it during the bar exam. Lord, please give me calmness. In Jesus' name, Amen."

Song: "My Hope is in You, Lord" by Aaron Shust

DAY 51

Final Weekend Before Bar Exam

DAY TWO

"To Study, or Not to Study?"

"In their hearts humans plan their course, but the
LORD establishes their steps."
—Proverbs 16:9 (NIV)

WHETHER OR NOT TO STUDY the final weekend before the bar exam is your personal decision based on how you feel, and what works best for you. The key is to be ready to face the Bar exam calm, rested, mentally and physically energized for the endurance testing. Therefore, do what feels right for you.

Consider what you really need. If not studying makes you worry, you may need studying to feel calm. If you feel "brain dead" and fatigued, you may need a weekend break to reenergize. Whatever the decision, make sure it's yours, not someone else's. Be content with it and do not chastise yourself. Scripture tells us that if we make poor decisions, God can establish our steps in such ways to make them right. The key is faith.

PRAYER:

"Dear Lord, I'm just having some trouble managing this stressful time in my life. The stress is getting to be too much for me, and I need your strength to get me through. I know you are a pillar for me to lean on in tough times. Lord, please order my steps. I know that I can do nothing right without your guidance and help; direct me by your wisdom and power, that I may pass the Bar exam so that it may be beneficial to me and others and to the glory of your holy name. In Jesus' name, Amen."

SONG: "Order my Steps" by Mississippi Mass Choir

DAY 52

Final Weekend Before Bar Exam

DAY THREE

"Stop! Don't Even Think it!"

"I can do all things through Christ which strengthens me."
—Philippians 4:13

A PERSON'S CONFIDENCE LEVEL IS ONE of the most reliable predictors of whether or not they will succeed in life. There are many people with extraordinary ability and intelligence who fails to carry out God's will for their lives because they lack confidence.

Stay positive. Discard negative thoughts. Remind yourself every day that you CAN pass the Bar exam. Cast out fear. Fear is the fuel that feeds anxiety. Positive affirmations are energizing.

Be cautious about comparing yourself to someone else. As you stand at the brink of your finish line, discard those "what ifs" and "I don't want to disappoint—." This isn't about anyone else. You are taking the bar exam for yourself and your calling. Concentrate on reaching YOUR goal. God looks to see how faithful you are in doing His will for YOUR life—not how your abilities measure up to someone else's. Choose to believe God's promises and let go of the past; let go of what others may think about you and whether you will meet their expectations.

Today, this very moment, claim the promise in Philippians 4:13 as your own. Just like Paul, declare you have the assurance of Christ's strength. Accept it by faith. Rather than letting fear and anxiety hold you back, move ahead in perfect confidence that you have God's sustenance, direction, and provision to fulfill anything He calls you to do.

You CAN pass the Bar exam.

PRAYER:

"Dear Lord, today I am just really stressed. You know, Lord, that I am going to the hotel tomorrow to be near my bar exam site, to start the bar exam testing process. I know it's probably not the biggest world problem at this moment, but, Lord, it's what I'm facing right now, and I need you in this time. I know that no problem is too big or too small for you to handle, and I need to turn this stress over to you to help me with. Thank you. In Jesus' name, Amen."

SONG: "Let's Go!" By Group 1 Crew featuring Toby Mac

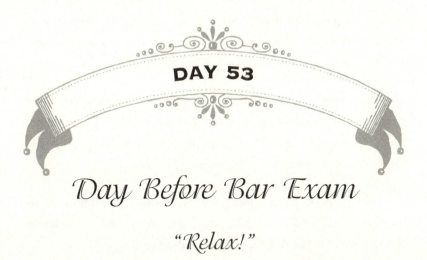

DAY 53

Day Before Bar Exam

"Relax!"

"What time I am afraid, I will trust in thee. In God I will praise His word, in God I have put my trust; I will not fear what flesh can do unto me"
—Psalm 56:3-4

THE DAY BEFORE THE START of the bar exam should be relaxing. Relaxing for one person may be taking the day off, while for another it may be cruising through some outlines or practice tests. Do what feels best for you. Runners, however, lay off the day before a marathon race. You are as prepared as you're going to be at this point. A few extra hours will likely just exhaust you before the big day.

God has assigned you to do this. There is no reason to be faithless or scared. You CAN pass the bar exam!

PRAYER:

"Lord, thank you for all the blessings you have placed in my life. Thank you for being with me during this time when I feel a bit overwhelmed. Thank you for always being there and allowing me to rely on you. Lord, I am so worried and anxious about my bar exam.

Sometimes, I am scared at the thought of the Bar exam and I lack confidence in my own wisdom and understanding. Lord, you promised to give wisdom and understanding to those who ask you. So, I ask you for wisdom and understanding. I request your favor.

Lord, please forgive me for all the time I wasted and forgive all my shortcomings. I totally rely upon you, Lord. I know I can do all things through Christ who strengthens me! So I depend on you.

Be with me while I write my Bar exam essays tomorrow, and hold my hand! Give me memory recall as I spot issues and write black letter law. Keep me in good health and peace so that I can do well on my exams. Thank you for helping me, Lord. I claim success in your mighty name. Lord, I know I CAN pass the Bar exam! In Jesus' name, Amen."

SONG: "My Hope Is Built on Nothing Less"

DAY 54

Bar Exam

DAY ONE

"Release Fear"

"For God hath not given us the spirit of fear; but of power,
and of love, and of a sound mind."
—2Timothy 1:7

GOD HAS NOT GIVEN US the "spirit of fear" but He has given us three things that will help us overcome fear: The spirit of power, the spirit of love, and the spirit of self-control. Conquering fear is not a consequence of personal determination; rather, a dependence on a trusting and loving God. In Christ you can conquer your fear of the bar exam today if you have a personal relationship with Him.

Praying before an important exam enables you to gain perspective on your life. Again, God has assigned you to do this. There is no reason to be faithless or scared. You can pass the bar exam!

Morning Prayer for
First Round of Exams:

"Dear Heavenly Father,

I finally made it to this point in my marathon to the bar exam! I have been diligently preparing for this very day, Lord. Help me walk into the bar exam center this morning with just a little or no nervousness. Give me the peace that passes all understanding. When it is all said and done, I will know that I walked in and did my best.

Lord, I pray for your guiding hand as I take the first round of exams, and I ask for calmness when I walk out of the exam center. Please be with me. After this morning's exam, help me to let go of the questions and possible answers. Help me to refrain from researching through my notes to see if I answered a question correctly. It only serves to cause me more anxiety. I want to let go of the first round, not discuss the test with anyone, nor relive it in my thoughts or actions. Lord, I know I can pass the Bar exam! In Jesus' name, Amen."

SONG: "Praise Him In Advance" by Marvin Sapp

Afternoon Prayer for
Second Round of Exams:

"Dear Lord,

As I take this Bar exam, I thank you that my relative worth is not based on my performance, but on your great love for me. Walk with me, Lord, through this challenging process. Bring back to my mind everything I studied and be gracious with what I have overlooked. Help me to remain focused and calm, confident in the legal analysis and in my ability to write clear, succinct sentences, and firm in the knowledge that no matter what happens today you are there with me. Lord, I know I can pass the Bar exam! In Jesus' name, Amen."

DAY 55

Bar Exam

DAY TWO

"Prayer Power"

"Pray without ceasing."—1 Thessalonians 5:17

PRAYER IS EMPOWERING. MUCH PRAYER, much power. Little prayer, little power. No prayer, no power. Stay connected to the power source. God has assigned you to do this. There is no reason to be faithless or scared. You can pass the bar exam!

Morning Prayer for First Round of Exams:

"Dear Lord,

Today, please give me a sharp sense of understanding, a retentive memory, and the ability to grasp things correctly and fundamentally.

Grant me the ability to be exact in my explanations, and the ability to express myself with sound legal reasoning. Dear Lord, I thank you that even though I may feel stress and pressure during this bar exam, you are a very present help. I have great expectations of receiving your strength today, Lord. Thank you, Heavenly Father. Lord, I know I can pass the Bar exam. In Jesus' name, Amen."

SONG: "Your Love Never Fails" by Newsboy

Afternoon Prayer for
Second Round of Exams:

"Dear Heavenly Father, Thank You for Your presence with me during our morning round of tests, and Your continued presence. Help me to believe that even as I am praying, you are giving me the wisdom and help I need for this afternoon's round of tests. Thank you for the ability to recall what I learned in my studies. I know the knowledge gained will be beneficial to me as it says in Proverbs: "He who gets wisdom loves his own soul; he who cherishes understanding prospers." (Proverbs 19:8 N) Lord, I know I can pass the Bar exam! In Jesus' name, Amen."

SONG: "When Mercy Found Me" by Rhett Walker Band

Bar Exam

LAST DAY

"Let it Go!"

Let your eyes look directly forward, and your gaze be straight before you.
Ponder the path of your feet; then all your ways will be sure. Do not swerve to
the right or to the left; turn your foot away from evil.
—Proverbs 4:25-27

IT IS THE LAST DAY of your bar exam. The previous days' exams are now history. Let them go. Do not place undue stress on yourself by retracing what you did or did not write or remember. Chances are you did better than you think. If you are right, what can you do about it now? Nothing. But you can live in the present and strive to do your very improving best on today's exam. Many people leave the bar exam with the feeling that they didn't pass, and then nearly pass out when they get the news that they did. Just assume you did as well as everyone else and let it go.

Continue to pray. Prayer forces us to take time out to spend some quiet time alone with God and our private thoughts. In prayer, we look towards God for strength and support. Again, God has assigned you to do this. Let go of yesterday, and previous unsuccessful bar exam scores. There is no reason to be faithless or scared. You can pass the bar exam!

Morning Prayer for
First Round of Exams:

"Dear Lord,

It's my last exam day! I am really exhausted. It may seem strange praying to you because of a Bar exam, but, right now, the Bar exam overshadows everything else going on in my life. Quite frankly, after yesterday's exams, I feel inadequate and am second-guessing myself. Lord, please help me let go of the previous days' exams because I have seen how stress, self-criticism, fear and anxiety affect my performance. I need your peace. I pray to you for the strength to handle the pressure that I feel.

Please give me the confidence to feel secure in my knowledge and preparation as I begin the first round of my last exam day. Give me the endurance and mental recall as I answer questions this morning. Lord, I know I CAN pass the Bar exam! In Jesus' name, Amen."

SONG: "One Thing Remains" by Kristian Stanfill

Afternoon Prayer for
Second Round of Exams:

"Dear Lord,

Please help me answer most of the questions on the afternoon's exam correctly. Give me memory recall and give me legal insight to recognize issues. Help me select the correct answer as it sits among many other choices that will *appear* to be the correct answer. I pray for discernment to overcome any trickery. I want to pass this exam, Lord. I know I CAN pass the Bar exam! In Jesus' name, Amen."

SONG: "I will Follow" by Chris Tomlin

DAY 57

Bar Exam

THE DAY AFTER

"Forget It!"

"Casting all your anxieties on him, because he cares for you."
—1 Peter 5:7 (ESV)

THE MARATHON FINALLY ENDED. THE bar exam is over. Assume you did as well as the next person, and forget it! Do not pass judgment on yourself, nor compare yourself to others' "after the bar" comments. Disassociate yourself from that energy. Keep in mind, you have just run a long, tedious, stressful race. Give thanks to God, ask that He guide the examiners toward a passing score for you, and forget it!

PRAYER:

"Dear Lord, enable me to trust in the good outcome of the bar exam. By Your Grace, I hope to crown my efforts with success. Thank You, Lord, for your presence in my life and this bar marathon journey. I love you, I trust you, I believe in you. In Jesus' name, Amen."

SONG: "Thank you Lord" by Mary, Mary

About the Author

Ida Tyree Hyche, Esq. is a practicing attorney licensed by the Alabama State Bar. After completing a successful career as a Human Resources leader for a major federal agency, and retiring as an Army Reserve Chief Warrant Officer, Tyree Hyche began her second career as an Attorney. She tithes her legal services through pro bono commitments, a personal faith-based promise she made during her bar exam studies. Tyree Hyche is a Christian leader who serves on several boards, has traveled internationally, and engages young people in training and development. Her personal motto is, "You can't complain if you don't train!" Tyree Hyche is currently International Editor for a successful global Christian missionary magazine reaching over 30,000 women missionaries, their friends, and families worldwide. She lives in Center Point, Alabama.

REVIEWS

"As a newly barred attorney I am well aware of the physical, emotional, and spiritual stress that studying for the bar exam can place upon an individual. Serenity Through The Bar Exam is an uplifting devotional, short and concise yet it provides the perfect amount of focus and spiritual nourishment that the mind and body need while on the grueling path to becoming a lawyer."

Amanda Duncan, Esq.
Member, Georgia State Bar

"This is a very helpful devotional even for those persons studying for intense licensing and exams, other than the bar. After looking back over the times that I spent studying for my Hebrew and Greek exams while pursuing my M. Div., I wish this book had been available to bring God's Word to life in my journey. This book is a testimony to the power, love and availability of God to everyone who will trust in Him as Lord and Savior."

Ruby Heard-Bustamonte, Masters in Divinity
Beeson Divinity School, Samford University

Made in United States
Orlando, FL
20 November 2023

39232890R00086